Nightmare in the Woods

By Christyne Anne

Dedications and Mentions:

My Husband: who makes me feel I can do anything. Thank you for being there for me and giving me the encouragement, I needed.

My Children: who think their EMT Mother is a hero.

My Foster Son and Grand children

My Creative muse Phil Morin and his lovely wife Renay.

And my Pen Pals and Fans.

And my Best friends Janice Kneeney , Arron Foss, and To The Mayer Fire Department

Thank you all. I hope this short Tale lives up to my creative works.

Introduction:

I never was much of a believer of the supernatural or Crytozoology. Cryptids were not a word in my vocabulary. I had heard many myths, folklore, tale tells, and legends in my life and if I think about it one would surmise those stories all have roots somewhere. I will also give you that in recent years some animals we thought were extinct were found to be living and doing well. The Mega mouth shark comes to mind as well as the Goblin Shark. Cyrtids differ for me only in they have never been proven to exist in the first place.

The legend of Bigfoot is the one I am most familiar with; I grew up about stories of Bigfoot when I lived in California. Bigfoot was featured in cartoons when I was a child. I read up on Bigfoot sightings, the subject fascinated me to no end. The number of sightings alone had me convinced these magnificent being must exist.

There were many people who came up with concepts of what these creatures as they called them were. My favorite is Bigfoot is just a hermit with long hair hiding in the woods to get away from other people. No kidding I heard that!

The Lockness Monster (Nessie) I have also heard of. Who has not? Nessie is one of Scotland's most notorious residents. Nessie the Monster of the Lock, how did she get in there? Was the creature born in the Lake? What Kind of Monster is Nessie?

The most common belief is that Nessie is a Plesiosaurus. There are others that believe she is just a large Sturgeon. A photo of Nessie from 1934 was later proven to be a hoax, further the lock has been searched many times over with no proof of Nessie. Still, it is fun to believe a creature long since believed extinct may still be lurking in the depths of the unknown.

Bigfoot and Nessie are the only two Cyrtids I have heard of until recently. I had heard many old folklore of deadly creatures and evil spirts that lurk in the night. Vampires, Werewolves, Ghost and Wendigos. Some are Urban Legends, some are mere myths, some have been handed down through Native Americans through the ages.

One term I had never heard before was the term Dogman. I had watched a documentary on "The Beast of Bray Road". Bray road is a quiet, rural road in Elkhorn Wisconsin. Sighting of the Beast date back as early as 1936; with a series of sighting in the 1980s and 90s. This lead a local reporter Linda Godfrey taking an interest in these sighting, a skeptic at first, she later came to believe the witness were telling the truth. This led to Godfrey's book "The Beast of Bray Road: Hunting the Wisconsin Werewolf".

I did not go searching for information on Dogman until after I had my terrifying second encounter. You will read about how close that encounter was and the fear it left behind in its wake. My research lead me to "DogmanEncounters.com!". I read through all the stories looking for one like mine. I found one so much like mine I nearly choked on the fear it invoked,

I also researched the books by noted Bigfoot writer Tom Lyon. The three-volume series had some of the most chilling tales I had read thus far. This series convinced me there may very well be something to these Dogman encounters. I was still having doubts about what I had seen, but after reading Lyon's accounts from people and how those descriptions met up to the being, I saw. I now feel sure what was stalking my old home was in fact a Dogman.

Chapter One: The First Encounter

These encounters took place over two-thousand miles from the rest, but it was noteworthy to add to my encounters with this mysterious beast. I was spending the summer in a small West Virginia town with my cousin Sara.

Sara's husband Nick worked nights as a paramedic for the local fire department. Sara and I were left alone with just their two Czechoslovakian German Shepherds Freya and Thor. Their home was located next a dirt road. The road was the only one in or out. The area was surrounded by heavy forest land. The house itself was just a single wide trailer sitting on five-acre lot. There was one barn, shed and the dog's kennel.

My cousin raised pigs, chickens and had a couple goats. The shed housed tools and the lawnmower. The dogs' kennel was used to house them when the couple was away. Freya tended to be a bit rowdy whenever they were gone, so to keep the large dog in check they kenneled her and Thor. Thor was a loveable pup still. Thor was Freya only pup from the litter before. All had been born healthy but the other five all died under usual, tragic, ways. Sara never explained. Just that it was also a part of building the kennel for the dogs. I just assumed it was a mountain lion or maybe a bear and it was just too painful for her to talk about.

I should probably tell you I was ten at the time and very adventurous. I would wonder the wilderness for hours. My favorite activity was vine swing. Sara always had me take Thor with me and I had to be in well before dark. I was young though and who really listens to anything when you are young and having a blast.

One day, I ventured further from the house than normal. Thor was happily trotting a head of me. I would stop every now and again to pick up treasures to take home. I liked to collect different size leaves for my artwork. I also would find rocks to paint on. Rocks are cheaper than canvas when you are first learning. Plus "Pet Rocks" were all the rage then.

We had been out a while when Thor stopped dead in his tracks. I could smell something horrid. I was young but could not relate the smell to anything I knew other than rotten hamburger. I started to get closer to the source but suddenly stopped. Thor seemed to snap out of his trance and started barking wildly at me, he was forcing me to go back. I remember telling him to "Shut up, I want to see." I tried to force my way around him. Thor held his stance. "Stupid dog let me pass." I insisted.

"Chris, Chris?!" I heard my name being called. I turned to where I heard the voices and froze. Thor came along my side barking wildly. There just off to the left sat back on its hind legs was the biggest dog I have ever seen! I tried not to scream or run. It tilted its large head to on side like it was studying me. It was bigger than I was at nearly five feet tall, light brown and white fur, it head was very much like the shepherd's by my side, it eyes were a weird yellowish colour, and it had arms and hand with sharp looking nails and not paws.

I heard my name being called repeatedly, but neither it nor I moved for what seemed like forever. Thor suddenly started toward it. The beast let out a low, deep growl. "It okay big guy the dog will leave you alone if you leave us alone." I told something I did not even know what was. The voices growing near drew its attention, it turned in the direction of the people heading our way. It turned back to me and then fled into the woods. The last I saw of it the huge dog was heading down the mountain side.

I sat down on a fallen tree and burst into tears. "What was that monster?" was it a mis-sharpen dog? What had Thor tried to stop me from seeing? Still crying, I got to my feet and walked down the path to see for myself what Thor would not had allowed. I was determined more than ever I was going to see what had caused him to stop.

The closer I got to the smell the worst it had gotten. I was sure I was going to throw up before I saw what was causing that stench. Nothing could have prepared me for what I had found. It was a den of some sort, with a hole dug down a bit but also kind like a shelter. I had seen animal dens before but this one was bigger. It still extremely hard to talk about it. There was a fresh kill inside, it looked like it might have been a piglet, maybe two. There was inside all over the den, old bones of other prey. I started crying again. It occurred to me then I might have been in real danger.

The hand on my shoulder made me jump and scream. "Easy Sweetpea" Nick cooed pulling me into his meaty arms. Sara husband was a hulk of a man at 6'8" but also just a big loveable, teddy bear. It also was a handsome man. Dark, rich, curly brown hair, handlebar mustache, sun kissed skin and light amber eyes that shined with mischief. He was one of the most loving people I had ever met. 40 years later, he has not changed a bit.

Nick picked me up into his massive arms trying to calm me. I was shaking so bad and fearful that beast would come back. Nick had not come alone though he had three firemen with him from his work. Michael, Jack, and Tyler. All four were fairly good size men. I should have felt safe but after seeing the den I felt anything but.

Tyler peered into the den I had found. "Nick, You guys have to see this." He said quietly. Tyler's tone was very neutral. The look on his young 20ish face was not. He looked frighten, my cousin's husband and the others looked inside.

"Man, I have never seen anything like that." Michael told Nick.

Nick nodded. "Me either and I been hunting this area for years." He cradled me closer to him. "Sweetpea you see whose house this is?"

"No Sir." I lied. I did not think they would believe me I saw a huge dog bigger than me. I was also scared if I told about the monster it would come for me. I was ten after all.

Nick carried me up the slope leading back to the house. I looked back and could swear I saw it again just a bit down from its den. It was watching us making sure we left its area.

Nick and his friend went back with shotgun and rifles to explore the den again. The entire den had been destroyed

I stayed close to the house after that. I was to frighten to venture beyond the barn were the animals were and never without the dogs. Sara kept a closer eye on me too. Nick told Sara about the den and that he was convinced I had saw something.

"She is a very mistrusting little girl," Sara had said. "Maybe she thinks she will get in trouble or simply whatever she tells us we won't believe."

My cousin had always been a bright spot in my life. Sara was the sweets, most gentle person I knew. Sara had been about 5'6', with long light brown hair, olive skin, nicely shaped with blazing, green eyes. She died suddenly in April of 1986. Sara left behind a heart-broken Nick and two beautiful children. The pure apples of their parent's eyes. Nick has yet to remarry. The devotion to their family and one another was the center of their lives.

Nick was quiet for a minute or two before saying, "Chrissy a smart little girl too and you did not feel the way she was quivering. Babe, Sweetpea saw something?"

"It may not have been that thing!" Sara Insisted.

I had heard enough at that point; I came around into the kitchen so they both knew I was there. I grabbed an apple and took a bite, "What thing?" I asked between bites.

Sara gave a weak smile and began dinner taking pork chops out of the fridge. "What sides do you want?" She asked us. Changing the subject.

"Not pork chops please!" I winced thinking of the piglet in the den. "just a salad with boiled eggs and cheese," I suggested

"This is not a restaurant '" She replied. "You eat what on your plate." Sara began to ready the chops. "If you would like to make a salad get the veggies out and help."

I took everything I needed out of the fridge and a huge bowl. I washed everything down and began tearing the lettuce up. "It was a Dog of some sort but much bigger." I told them.

The two of them looked at each other knowingly. Nick placed a hand over mine to stop me chopping. "How close was it to you?"

"You knew something like that was near here!" I accused glaring at them in turn.

"We have only seen it a couple of times." Sara explained trying to calm me. "We thought it only came out at night. We also think that is what got Freya puppies."

 "What is it?" I asked again

  Nick let go of my hand. "Depends on who you ask Sweetpea." He went on with his explanation. "Most people around here think it a White Wolf of some old folklore story and others think it is a Humm…. werewolf."

 "It was daylight. Werewolves don't exist, and I want to go home." I said holding up a finger for each.

"Comprise, you go down to Granny and Grampa's" Sara suggested" Until you are ready to come back and at least spend the day with me."

  I thought about it for a few seconds. I was not sure that I was not totally overreacting if I stayed in the house, I was safe. "Well, maybe I can stay a little longer."

Chapter Two: What is in the Woods


I decided to stay with my cousin because of our close bond. I rarely left the house. As much as it pains me to say it, I was frightened of this unknow beast. Time however does have a healing affect and soon the incident, the memory had begun to fade. Plus, being an outdoors person; I was restless inside. There was also the fact it did not try to eat me.

It must have been my restlessness that got me to agree to take some cornbread and pinto bean down Mrs. Lambert. She was a kindly, elderly, widow, who lived just down the road next to the post office. It was a short walk there and back, I thought it might help me get confidence back being outside the house.

It was a beautiful, summer day with the hint of the rain from the night before still lingering in the air. The road was lined with wild Roses, Daisy and Black Bettys or Sun Flowers. I have never been good at telling the two apart. There were also patches of Black Berries and Blue Berries growing along the mountain side. The many trees created a canopy giving just enough shade that the heat of the day was held at bay.

I strolled along admiring everything about this stunning little, country, town lost in thought. West Virginia is vastly different from my home in Arizona. Arizona this time of year is hot. It called a dry heat but it about 111 degrees or more in the summer. I pretty much love my home state any other time of the year.

The snap of a branch brought me back to reality with a jolt. The eerie feeling, I was being watch suddenly consumed me. I kept walking just picking up the pace a bit. I heard what I thought was heavy footsteps moving parallel to me. I stopped and looked around me. I did not see anything. I had this feeling that something was there, however. I resumed walking but remained alert to my surrounding. The monster of course came to mind. I was just the right size to be considered prey. I suddenly wondered if the reason it had not attacked during our last encountered because it had just had a meal or two from the looks of den. My mind was whirling with fear. The "What Ifs" coming by the dozens. I was rounding the post office when suddenly a wild turkey came screaming out of the woods like a 747 over my head. I did not even know they could fly until then.

I laughed; I had been followed by a turkey not some giant of a dog. I started to slow my pace again and just enjoy my time outside. I was walking up Mrs. Lambert's driveway when I happened to look out across the yard. There next to one of the trees, I saw it again. It was just watching me. It made no move to advance towards me, it was just staring at me. Our eyes locked. I could not move or breathe. What is that thing? Why would it not leave me alone?

Mrs. Lambert had been watching for me and suddenly opened the door. I jumped back startled and gave a little scream.

"Oh dear," The kind lady said. "I did not mean to give ya a scare." With a little chuckle motioning me to come in. I turned back to where the creature had been. It was gone. "Something wrong girl?"

"No Ma'am." I answered following her inside.

Mrs. Lambert had a tray of sandwiches, two china teacups with a matching teapot. The sweet lady's home was modest, but nicely furnished. She had a nice Rose pattern sofa and matching chair. A china hutch with the same china design as the cups and pot on the tray on her Queen Anne coffee table. The end table were also Queen Anne style, there was an old-style rocker with a Rose pattern cushion that matched the sofa and chair and just off to the side a small piano.

Mrs. Lambert seemed to be watching me as she pour my tea. "It is Earl Grey," handing me my cup. "I added the sugar and cream for you." She smiled warmly. "I am just so happy to be receiving." She looked it too. "Not many folks want to visit an old woman."

"Thank you." I answered politely taking the cups. "Did you make the cushion yourself?" I found it odd everything matched some perfectly my curiosity got the best of me.

She smiled warmly," Yes, Good eye." She commented incredibly pleased. "It took nearly two months, but I did indeed.

I sipped my tea. "You play the piano?"

"No not anymore." She replied sadly. Mrs. Lambert offered a sandwich to me. "They are Cucumber Sandwiches. My mother came over from England in the 1800s."

I took a sandwich and bit in genteelly in case I did not like it, but found it was delicious. "These are really good." I told her.

"Thank you Dear." Mrs. Lambert said. "It is nice to hear that."

I sipped my tea and nibbled my sandwich. "What part of England was your mother from?"

"Stafford, in Staffordshire. I get the feeling you are in no hurry to get home?" She suggest with a deeply, pleasant smile." Are you sure you want to visit with me?"

The question caught me off guard. I guess it may seem strange to an elderly woman a ten-year-old was willing to stay and chat. I admit she was genuinely nice. She was a small, slip of a thing, with her hair bound up in a bun at her nape. She wore a modest dress of dark blue that matched her eyes. Mrs. Lambert had a small pert, little nose combined with a stubborn chin "Yes Ma'am, you seem like a fascinating lady. I bet you have seen something in your life." I explained honestly.

"Oh, my but aren't you a sweet child." She exclaimed with a note of thrill in her voice "Yes, I suppose I could tell you a tale or two if you have time."

"I just need to call Sara to come get me." I told Mrs. Lambert. There was no way I was walking back to the house with that thing outside on the prowl. It was safer to call Sara than risk walking back. It true this creature had not hurt me, but it might be sizing me up and the thought unnerved me. Sara was a safe bet for a way home.

It took me a while to realize my elderly host had gone silent. She was white as a ghost to boot. I turned to where she was staring. Just outside her window was the monster. I tried not to scream. It was just watching us. A sort of smile on its face.

"It is okay Dear." Mrs. Lambert whispered. "It never tries to come inside the house."

I whipped my head around to face her again. "How often do you see that thing!" I cried and it let out an unholy growl that sent chills down my spine.

"It doesn't like loud noises or sudden movements." She told me, "You need to be calm Dear. You show it fear, it gives you more."

"I want to call Nick to come get me please?" I begged nearly in tears as it growled again louder.

"Yes, I think we should call someone." She agreed when it started testing doors. "Phones just inside the kitchen."

I walked slowly into the kitchen and dialed Nick at his fire department. I waited as it rang and rang.

"Hello, Antelope Fire Department." A man's voice answered.

"Hi, I need to speak with Nick Summers, It an emergency."

It must have been the sheer panic in my voice that prompted him to ask. "What kind of emergency Sweetheart, where are you?

"I am not sure." I admitted. The kitchen door rattled then, and I screamed into the phone a blood curding ripping one.

"Calm down Sweetheart. "He instructed "Just let me help you."

The doorknob continued to rattle. Panic filled my entire being. "Just get me Nick Summers please. I need my cousin's husband."

I was near to tears now and he could tell. "Just a sec Sweetheart don't hang up."

A few second later Nick's welcoming voice came on the phone "Nick Summers, how can I help you."

"Nick, it is Chrissy" I spilled out still in tears. "It is here." Was all I could choke out.

"What is here?" he asked concern filling his voice.

"The monster." I told him simply. "It is trying to get inside the house."

"We will be right home Sweetpea." He assured me. "Is Sara okay?"

"I am not at home I am at Mrs. Lambert's just down the road. Sara had me bring some things down for her. I saw it on the way here, but it went back into the woods. Then Mrs. Lambert saw it watching us from the window and now it is trying to get into the house. She said it does not like loud noises and I screamed and made it mad." I rushed out.

"Okay Sweetpea you have to calm down okay?" Nick's voice tried to smooth me and talk me down." We will be there shortly.

You two hide somewhere it safe until we get there." He said and hung up.

I went back to Mrs. Lambert, told her the plan. She suggest a linen closet area where there was no windows or doors. We hid there and waited until help arrived. It seemed like forever before there was a knock on the door. I asked Mrs. Lambert to stay put while I made sure it was Nick. It was. I opened the door and threw myself into his waiting arms.

Nick insisted we both be checked out my paramedics. There were ambulances in case either of us needed one. Fish and Game and the local Sheriff's department were there too. I gave a report to both as the medics worked on me. I told them what I had seen, where I had seen the monster etc. I was still a little worked up. The paramedic told Nick my Blood Pressure was up and pulse was beating too fast. He wanted to take me to the hospital, Nick nodded. I knew they thought I was in shock, psychosocially. Mrs. Lambert was taken to the hospital too. She had been just as frighten as I had been, but I would not be staying in that home alone if that thing came back again.

Sara sent me down to my Grandparent's as soon as I got out of the hospital. I had terrible nightmares. I woke up screaming about werewolves every night. It was decided a week later I should return to Arizona. The place I had once thought of as a piece of Heaven now had a nightmare image attacked to it.

Mrs. Lambert ended up moving in with her daughter. She was left just as traumatized as me

Chapter Three: Phoenix Arizona (The Ordinary Life)

My early experiences with the unknow canine had long since been all but forgot. I had occasional nightmare, but they were vague at best. I guess it was leftover PTSD from my encounters. It hard to say for sure. I was so young when those sightings took place. The events seemed unreal to be as an adult, with adult logic.

In my mind's eye what I saw was just a big dog. Granted it was much bigger than any known breed, but still it was a dog of some sort. It was certainly not a werewolf. I still refused to entertain the idea any creature resembling a werewolf could exist and there not be a big media frenzy to locate it. Hunters would be rummaging about the forest searching for their trophy of a lifetime, cryptologist would be desperate to its existence, and scientist would be eager to debunk whatever evidence was found. Scientist would try to find some logical explanation even if the facts were overwhelming. It just how thing are. It was better just to not believe such a monster could be real. The logic of an adult woman who had had the shit scared out of her.

I moved to Arizona in the early 1980s. We moved to Arizona from upstate Virginia. The contrast was shocking. My parents, younger brother and I moved to the greater Phoenix area for my Dad's work. I was used to wide opened spaces, riding my horse every day, going swimming in the nearby creek, and enjoying the great outdoors.

Phoenix was crowded, loud, houses set one on top of each other and were basically all the same style. Phoenix lacked charm and its own character from my point of view. I was not happy living in Phoenix. It was not until a snow trip with my volleyball trip to Flagstaff I discovered the whole state was not one great big desert.

Arizona has much to offer for people who like the outdoors life like I do. Flagstaff reminded me much of West Virginia with its large population of pine trees and greenery. Some of the homes were like the German style ones I saw when I visited my Mother in Europe. My team had stayed at a cute lodge and it snowed the entire time we were there. The lodge was just a rustic A Frame, the rooms were dorm like, with six girls per room.

Arizona is home to the San Francisco Peaks. The peaks are formed from volcanos. The tallest peak is Mt. Humphreys Peak at about 12,633 feet in elevation. Humphreys usually has snow on its cap. Coconino County also offers the Grand Canyon, Bill Williams' mountain in the Williams area. You will find the Polar Express tour during Christmas time riding the rails from Williams to the Grand Canyon. There are many canyons to explore there and places for hiking and fishing.

Wildlife as such is plentiful, there are Elk, Black bears, Pronghorn, Bald Eagles, Prairie Dogs, Blue heron, and Mountain Lions. Just to name a few. Coyotes, squirrel, Rattle snakes (snake in general) can be found throughout much the state.

Heading south Sedona, Stoneman lake, Mormon Lake, are points of interest. Mormon and Stoneman are Arizona two natural lakes. The two lakes depths vary, but rarely exceed 10ft. Mormon sometimes dries up completely; However, the area is still breathtaking. An astray of wildflowers grow where the lake's underground water feeds them. There are cabins to rent for a nice getaway.

Sedona is stunning with its red rock formations, most notably Bell Rock, Cathedral rock and Boynton Rock. These magnificent butts are a part of the Vortex Tours Sedona has become known for during the New Age movement of the 1980s. It is held that these vortex have mystical energies. Sedona also has Slide Rock National Park. Nature's idea of a water side park. The slides are fed by Oak Creek Canyon, the swift moving water makes for a fun day in the Arizona heat. It was on my snow trip and later when I married my husband William, I saw what exactly Arizona had to offer and now would not want to live anywhere else.

. I met William in high school playing a game of football. Will's easy-going nature stole my young heart. We were a year apart in age, Will had been born the year after I was, but I did not care I wanted him for my boyfriend. Will had not wanted me then. He literally dated all my friends but me. It was heartbreaking then, today after twenty-seven years of a great marriage it is a funny story.

I had wondered at the time why he was not attracted to me. It was true, I was the hardcore, overachieving, honor, student to his laidback come what may. Will still got great grades. He also liked to party with my younger brother. The two gave new mean to the term "Young and Stupid" I cannot even begin to list the adventures the duo had.

We did hang out with the same crowd of people. It was a group of about twenty people or so. It was a rowdy bunch of outcaste just chilling out together because we had no other groups to click with. High school is unfortunately like that. Sometimes you just do not fit in, however we somehow made it work with our vastly different personalities'.

Will and I began dating in 1992, we both were staying with our parents. Our parent's house were a street apart. I had dropped by a week before he asked me out, but his Mom said he was out with his Dad on a hunting trip. I felt so disappointed. She told him when he got home," Some little girl stopped by to see you." The problem of being twenty-five and looking sixteen. I like that now that I am in my fifties!

We met up a week later at the polling booths of all places. He asked me out right then and there. I of course said yes. Our romance was whirlwind and five months later we were married. A little over four months we had our first child, a little girl named Mary. Mary was our light and joy. She was such a good baby. Mary rarely cried, always was all smiles and began growing too fast for this Mom.

Mary was talking by five months, began walking at seven months. She was just baring through life too fast for Mom to keep up. She was always wanting to learn new things too. I was surprised when she was born, Mary took more after me, deep olive skin, hazel eyes, little adorable nose, and high cheek bones. Mary's hair was all her Daddy's reddish, brown with curls delight.

Mary's first birthday we decide to try for a second and finally baby. We did not have to wait long. We went on a trip at the end of November to a little Bed and Breakfast in the Prescott area and came home to Phoenix pregnant with baby Jennifer.

My pregnancy with Jenny did not go easy, by the fourth month I was on complete bed rest. If my feet hit the ground, it was not long before I had labor pains. I sent five months laying on my left side being waited on by my Stepmother Clare. It was hellish, I worried about our baby constancy. I was so frightened she would have problems or be born too soon. It kept me up at night and I was always crabby as a result. I do not know how anyone handled being around me at all those four long months.

Jenny came into this world right on time. Labor with her had been pathetically easy in contrast to Mary. The drugs they had given me with Mary had messed with my head and labor had been a nightmare. Jennifer's went like clockwork and completely drug free. I remember the doctor asking me if I thought she was bigger than her sister. I replied, "Beyond a doubt."

The little room I was in was packed with Grandparents, Will, and Mary, No one wanted to miss out on Jennifer; s birth. The family was eager to welcome the newest addition, then everything fell apart.

Two nurses brought in a crash cart, My heart plummet. "What was wrong?" I felt choked by the panic raising in me. "Was my baby in danger, was she dying before she was even born?" I wondered my mind whirling. "Was it me? Was I dying?" The doctors looked graved. No one was telling me anything, just to push. I felt medicine entering my system as monitor began sounding. The medications were hard to fight against. I did though and was rewarded by the sounds of my daughter's first cry.

The room had been emptied out at some point, it was just William and I (Nurses and Doctors), the nurse placed Jennifer in my arm. She was turning bluer my the second, her breathing was like a small kitten's meow. "Oh my God." I cried "She is dying, please don't let my baby die!" The nurse took her from me, and a team began CPR as they raced her to the neo-ICU or NICU. Tears poured from my face; my baby might not make it. The reality was more than I could bare.

What I was not aware of was I was not doing to hot myself. I had lost too much blood and was continuing to do so. The doctors tried to slow the bleeding. My husband had gone with Jenny as far as he could, then turned back to let me know how she was. He said he entered the room the nurse told him I needed a blood transfusion, or I might die. He said he had held my frail, limp hand to the ICU. He later said going home that night had been the worst experience of his life. He did not know if by morning he would have a wife or his new daughter.

The next morning, I woke up, weak, feeling very tired, but I wanted to know if my baby had made it. I was told she was in the NICU and doing better. I wanted to see her of course, I was told the doctor needed to see me first to get consent for a blood transfusion.

The first time I saw Jennifer, I was amazed by the sheer size of her. I had long since held the belief she was going to be bigger than Mary, but she looked humongous. I was told she was a nine-pound, five-ounce baby. Mary had been seven - and pounds twelve - ounces.

The flaming red hair, pale, cream, white, milk, skin, huge blues, set in the chubbiest, Cherub like face. She looked so perfect! She also resembled her father up one way and down. I asked to feed her. The moment I held her in my arms, she began screaming like a banshee. I knew then she would be simply fine. We would all be fine. Our family was completely.

William won a trip to Las Vegas later that year. It was part of a goal to get the guys in his shop to work toward putting out more successful parts in a timely matter. My husband has superior work ethic and won hands down.

A few weeks later, I started feeling sick. I was throwing up four or five times a day, I thought I had the flu since I did not miss my monthly misery. I literally fell off the exam table when the doctor told me I was pregnant…again! It had not even been a year! What was I going to tell Will, we had taken three steps to prevent pregnancy? Would my husband be happy or filled with dread like myself? The last time had not gone well. The memory had yet to even begin to fade.

I started to tell Will about our new baby about a half dozen times, but the nagging thought he would be upset kept my mouth shut. I did not try to make excuse for being sick either. Will notices I was incredibly sad too, but I said nothing. It took nearly three weeks before I decided to just call him at work and drop the bomb.

I had dialed his work asked for Will and when he came on the line "I am pregnant again" I told him numbly.

The phone dropped. I could hear people around him calling his name, Will repeating the single word "Three"

Someone Congratulated him on having triplets!


My last pregnancy was closely monitor. On the way to the ultrasound to check our baby sex.

"Boy or Girl?" Will asked

"Sorry Love," I answered. "Other girl"

He smiled knowingly. "What should we name this bundle of joy?"

"We were going to name our boy James," I suggested with a tone of mischief. "I was thinking her name should be Jamie. Jamie Lee after our favorite Queen of Scream."

"I like it." He said simply.

Our Jamie was born a few months later. She was perfectly health and looked just like her mother. Same auburn hair, same hazel eyes, high cheekbones, pert nose, dark olive skin. She was me reborn. My mini me. She was also a devoted Daddy's girl from the word go.

Our family settle into a nice little life. I never felt so complete before that point in my life. William worked and I stayed home to care for our girls. I tried going back to work but either Jennifer or Jamie would run the sitter out the door in record time. Jennifer was starting to show behavioral issues and Jamie just did not like anyone that was not family, even then she was fussy. She took an instance disliking to my brother. I will not say which one. I will say, she still does not like him.

In 2000 My little family moved from Phoenix to a small rural community in Yavapai County. This is where the Dogman and I met again

Chapter Four: Yavapai County

May 2013


William and I had separated in 2006. It is difficult so say what exactly what happened. It seems mundane now. It had nothing to do with how much we loved each other. It was more we are two vastly different people. Basically, we want the same things but it how to go about achieving that we sometimes disagree on.

Jennifer's care was the central part of many of those arguments. Jenny's behavioral outburst had become quite the thorn in my side. It was not her fault though, we learned Jennifer had suffered brain damage during her birthing of her frontal lobe. This is the part of the brain that controls behavior and self -control. Jenny is very much a right this second type of person. It must be now! She has mellowed with treatment and age.

I disagreed about putting her on heavy medications at the tender age of six. I was dead set against it. It appeared to me; she could be taught better self-control than medicated to the gills. I was not willing to give an inch either.

There was also the not so minor fact many people felt I was a terrible mother because of her behavior and my complete lack of ability to handle her. This was true to a point. I was working against not only her father, but both set of grandparents as well. They all lived in fear of telling her "NO!" I felt it was the only way she would learn. I rarely gave into her drama.

It did not help either the police were called multiply times for her by school official, neighbors', and such. It also was upsetting having Child Protection Services investigated us often. There was never anything found of course, still it put a stain on our marriage and me as a young mother.

I fell into a deep depression. I met a nice older woman name Mae through Jenny. Jenny and her great – Grand Daughter Lilly were best friends then and baby Jamie and I often went over for coffee before beginning our morning chores. It was a fast, easy going relationship.

Mae had traveled the world with her late husband, she learned to fly her own airplane in her fifties, been part of search and rescue in Alaska. She had the most amazing experience and tales to tell. She was also very out- spoken and self-assured. I grew very fond of her in a short time. Plus, unlike many people in the tiny rural community she was not judgmental about Jenny.

Will did not like Mae, he strong believed she was a bad influence on me. I had rarely been confrontational before, but suddenly I let my views be known. I felt it would help us work together to solve our problems. It made things worst.

I kept the housework up all week long, I took care of our children, clean house, washed clothes, and had his dinner waiting. (expect the time I caught the oven on fire) It was exhausting but I took pride in our home. I only took an hour a day to relax with Mae.

One Saturday morning I had wanted to go for coffee and visit Mae, I had Jamie all dress and ready to go. William threw a fit. I needed the down time. It had been a stressful week.

"If you walk out that door." He warned "I will have your things packed and you can get out."

It made me angry he would say something like that. I slammed the door on my way out. William threw all my stuff on the porch. When I got home two Police Office and Paramedics were there and I spend Christmas in a Psych ward.

Normally, I am very forgiving, but not this time. My 72 hours turned into a six month stay at a residential site for people who are Seriously Mental Illness. The test the psych doctors did on me showed I was both Bipolar and Schizoaffective. I already guessed I was Bipolar, but a form of Schizophrenia was like a dead sentence at first, I had this image of a drooling mess at the state hospital. There were no positive role models for Schizophrenia I knew of.

I voluntary went into this housing arrangement.  The plus side when I had enough of their crap, I called Mae and moved in with her. At first, I was not sure what to do with myself. I decided once I was stable to go back to work as an Emergency Medical Technician. The problem my certs were all elapsed. I had to go back to college to get recertified in emergency medicine.

It was towards the end of the term; I had taken the night class. I have never been much of a morning person once I began my medications. The medications made for a rough start every morning. It took me a good three hours to get my head on fairly well.

Anyways, I had stayed late to help a fellow student study for the final and our skills testing, so I was getting home later than usual. I drove a 1997, Tan, F150 Ford. It was about eleven pm as I was heading down our neighborhood road near the bridge. Just before where I turned toward our drive, a group of deer suddenly came bursting out of the bushes like they were fleeing from something. I hit my brakes to allow them to pass. A big buck bring up the rear turned its head back to the way they had been fleeing from and bam right into the nose of my truck. Knocked the poor thing stupid, the next thing I know this hair, black, arm with long nails like a racoon picks it clean off my truck's nose and take a huge bit into its neck. Blood spatter all over my truck and ground. I could not even breathe, I just watched in horror.

It was dark out and no moon, but I could make out a shape to some degree. It had a huge snout, pointed ears, its head reminded me of a German Shepherd's or Wolf's. As it picked the deer up into its meaty arms, it rolled its reddish eye back at me. It was unnerving this monster did it too. Like it was sending a silent message.

I watched it this being walk away, stunned in and in shock. It had to be at least six feet tall or more. I could see it holding the still fighting buck in its jaws, carrying the poor thing in those huge arms and it was head towards the bridge to home.

Scared to hell and back, I slammed my f-150 into reverse and zipped backward back the way I had come. I am so lucky no other drivers had been coming in that direction. It would have made for a bad accident. I drove to the gas station two miles away and tried to calm myself. I could not. This was a being I had seen as a child and just as terrifying as an adult. I felt just as helpless, just as frighten and powerless against something so massive.

I did what any married woman scared out of her wits would do, I called my husband. The panic in my voice told him something was wrong.

"Can I stay with you tonight?" I asked still shaking like a rattle snake.

There was a pause. "The kids have all gone to bed." He had answered

When I visited, I usually slept in the girl's rooms next to Jamie. My little mini me. Jamie may be a Daddy's Girl, but she also get Mommy pretty well and seems very in tuned with my emotions.

"I would rather sleep with you." I stated. Yes, I needed to feel safe. I would check in on my girls, make sure their windows were all closed up tight and they too were safe. "Will be coming in hot Babe, please leave the door open and meet me there."

Again, a pause. "Are you sure you are okay." He replied with his voice dipping with concern. "You sound terrified."

"Just be ready for me okay." I hung up and broke the speed limited to his house, blasted into his drive as close to the house as I could get, parked, and bolted into the house, slammed, and locked the door. I was like a mad woman on fire.

Once I checked the girls, I went and curled up in Will's big arms and started shaking again.

"What has you so scared?" Will demanded holding me close as I began to cry. I never answered him that night or any other. I did not want another trip to the Psych Hospital.

The next morning William was getting ready to leave for work and shook me awake. "Did you hit something with your car?"

"Huh?" I questioned have asleep still. "What did you say?" rubbing my eyes and letting out a sigh.

"Did you hit something with your car last night?" William repeated very testy.

I tried to focus on him. It had taken me until nearly dawn to finally find some shut eye. Images of the beast tortured my brain. "Oh yeah, no it hit me." I remember the buck slamming into the side of the trucks nose.

"What?" Will demanded angry now. "Was it a bear?"

"No, it was a big buck, it was running from," I stopped talking. What was I going to say a werewolf? Can you say Psych ward!!!

"From a bear!" he insisted loudly dragging me outside to show me the front end of my truck.

On the front of my F-150 he pulled out some long, string black and grey hairs. "These are not from a deer." He stated flatly "Hit a deer huh?" clearly not believing me

I walked over to the upper, driver's side of the nose, there was a dent from the deer. I showed Will. He was clearly shocked. "Okay start from the beginning."

I took the chance and told him the truth. What had happened, where and when. He stared at me in sheer debrief before saying "Babe, you could have been dog chow."

This was not the reaction I had been excepting. William actually believed me! You could have blown me over with a small dust devil. William ushered me back into the house. He brew us up some coffee, while I cooked us and the girls some breakfast, he called off at work stating a family emergency. I enjoyed this time with our girls.

We took them to the bus stop, keeping them in the car until the bus came and returned back to his house. I really did not think of it as our anymore. William and the girls made it their home. There was not even a picture of mama anywhere. It broke my heart.

Will pour me a cup of coffee and we sat down on the sofa together. He took my hand and those familiar butterflies dance in my stomach. We looked into each other's eyes for a long moment before I broke contact, I was ready to cry for what we had lost.

Will grew profoundly serious. "What I am about to tell you is just between us, I signed a wavier to never speak of this to anyone."

I nodded my understanding.

Chapter Five: Incident at Christopher Creek

It is important to give you an idea of where this even took place.

Christopher Creek is located in Gila County Arizona at the base of

the Mogollon (pronounced muggy own) Rim. The Mogollon Rim

is two-hundred miles long and anywhere from 5,000 ft. to 7,000 ft

in elevation. The Rim is where high desert meets just desert.

Christopher Creek sits in the desert part. It has a nice, cooling creek near by and about twenty-five or so camping sites. It a nice place to camp and enjoy the Great Outdoors.

Now, Arizona has its own Monster. The Mogollon Monster is said to be over seven-foot-tall, large reddish eyes, black and red fur except on its face, chest, hands, and feet. Its footprints measure about 22 inches in length, and it has the smell of decaying Peat Moss (Whatever that is)

The creature has been known to stalk around campgrounds, traveling from the Payson area to the Prescott area. This is just under one hundred miles by vehicle. It said to mimic other animals like birds, coyotes, and even the sounds of a woman in distress to lure prey. Some say it howls are bone chilling and echo through the night, it is known to be a nocturnal being. It also an omnivore, territorial and can be extremely violent. This is what is said of the Mogollon Monster.

Now what my husband told me did not quite add up to what happened to him and his friends on their trip in 1989. William's tale was vastly different in some minor details. This is what he told me that day in 2013.

William and his buddies were home on leave from the Army, they had just spent the last year at an undisclosed base he could not talk about nor could he say what they had been doing. This was pretty much the early part of our marriage as well. I hardly knew where he was or if I would be getting a phone call.

Anyways, the group was the usual guys, Will's best friend Bart,
Tomas, Larry, and Davis. The Group had decided to take a
drinking, camping trip near Christopher Creek.

Will took a huge gulp of coffee before launching into his hellish
tale. "We got to the campground around five pm. The place was
jammed packed." He began "We were all wiped out from the drive
so decided to hike back a ways and just chill out and party."
I nodded for him to continue.

"So, we hiked back about an hour or so, found a spot and set up
our tents for the night.  It was getting dark by the time we finished
setting up. Bart had been cooking us some grub and we cracked
open our beers and just enjoyed."

"Sounds about right." I thought of William and his friends. The
five of them were a rowdy bunch to be sure. The stories I could tell
you. Especially from Bart and Will alone. The two had enlisted in
the Army together. Somehow, they also always managed to get the
same orders to the next assignment. The man was a torn in my side
sometimes. He knew Will better than I did. There were times I
would get so jealous of their relationship. Petty as it sounds.

Will said they five of them had been getting pretty tanked when
suddenly one of them noted the forest around them had become
noticeably quiet. There is all kinds of wildlife in the area, coyotes,
bears, mountain lions, owls, bats, crickets, etc... If you have ever

been out at night you know what I mean, but Will said it was dead silence!

The guys started hearing sounds coming off to their left, low menacing growls with grunts and a chipping sound. He compared to when I make a chuckling sound with my tongue when I am in deep thought.

"Nice comparison Buddy" I shook my head

"The creepy part Hon," William struggled to keep his voice calm. I could tell the memory alone was terrifying him. I knew how he felt. "Something began answering it sounds."

Will claimed that before they knew it, two huge Wolf -like creatures came out of the forest towards the group. He said he nearly peed himself. The five of them were so frighten not a single one of them could move at first.

Will describe the Wolf-Creatures as being over seven feet tall. One had the blackest fur he had ever seen, was built like a body – builder. "It was heavy muscles." He told me with a mental shrug. I could see the panic on his face. I wondered if I had looked like that the night before. "It had the freakiest red, glowing eyes. Its claws were like long nails."

"The other one looked to have black and silver fur, smaller and it had a pair of breast." Holding his hand out to show the size. William went on with what he was saying. "The female was I believe smiling at us or smirking. It was a pure evil grin too." Will gave a physical shake as what appeared to be a chill ran down his spine.

"What did the two do next?" I questioned feverish to hear the rest of his experience.

"The two began to circle us." He explained the rest in a depth detail that was shocking. "We were all starting to panic. I cannot speak for the others, but I was pretty well lit. My mind refused to believe what I was seeing. I couldn't move and could barely breathe." Will shook his head in disgust. "We didn't have but out handguns with us and we knew that was not going to stop these things. I wanted to cry. I was convinced these being were about to devour all five of us."

"I can just imagine the fear you must have felt." I relied tenderly grasping his hand tightly. "I about made puddles too."

"Sweetheart, these thing were tightening their circle on us when gunfire erupted." Will told me, shocking the hell out of me.

"But you said you only had handguns, and you didn't think they would do much good." I repeated what he said to him. "Which one of you fired the shot?"

"It was not one of us Baby." He replied, "It was these guys in Military like uniforms. They chased them off and away from us.

We were told to leave our shit and follow them out. We were taken to two Hummers and then to a local police station."

"What?!" I exclaimed in pure shock. "Why were they there? I guess it was lucky for the five of you." I admitted.

William shifted uneasy next to me. "I don't think it had anything to do with luck. I think they were there hunting those things." He said, frankly. "In fact, I am sure of it."

"That a bit of a far stretch don't you think?" I questioned him full of doubts. Will let go of my hand and moved away from me a bit and took my face in his hands. "We were kept in the police station for hours, just strewing before a man in a suit came in and questioned each of us. He asked us all to sign a waiver and never speak to anyone about what we had seen." William told me bluntly. "Do you hear me no one must know what I have just told you."

All I could do was nod as I digest what William had just told me. The Government knew of these creature?!

Chapter Six: What Goes Bump in the Night

Mae's neighborhoods is important to mention so you can better understand the layout and isolation of the area. Mae's house was one of three on her street. The little street had one road in and out. There is dense desert scrubs lining both sides and a creek that runs along the back part of the property. The homestead sat on a two and half acre lot.

My experience left me feeling very shaken. I remember my earlier experiences and I was terrified of this unknow creature. Part of me tried to believe it was just a bear I had seen. Granted a mis-sharpen ugly bear but just a bear, nonetheless. My mind refused to accept what it may have seen. I had to tell myself serval times a day that werewolves did not exist.

Mae's house is a nice two-story, brown, brick with a wrap-around porch, and a screen-in Arizona room. It has a loft apartment with its own entry way and its own balcony attacked to it. The balcony has a tiny gate that leads off on to the roof to give assess to any work that may be needed done.

I was staying down stair in the room just off Mae's at the time of my encounter. Mae and I began to hear strange noise at night. A low growl, huffing noises, unusual muttering sounds and we both thought we heard walking on the roof tops. Mae was convinced it had to be a Puma (cougar) or perhaps a bobcat as we had run in with both before.

This was different though; I could feel it. It what I was no longer hearing at night that had me anxious. I did not hear the Horn Owl in the tree, the calls of Coyotes, the sounds of tree frogs along the creek bed nor even the hum of a cicadas. It was weird for no sounds to be heard at night, Nighttime met play time for many of the animals as they hunted, mated, and did animal things. Sheer quiet was just damn right creepy.

I went out for a smoke one night and had the odd sensation of being watched. It consumed my entire being, I perked my ears up a notch or two to hear. Nothing! I started taking a flashlight with me and scanning the area before I let my cigarette. There were a few times when I heard rustling in the brush near the house, but I never saw anything.

Spring was turning into Summer, when Mae's decided she needed a bit more income to fix up her home. She interviewed a number of people for the loft apartment. The one woman she did like was just a few years younger than her. Mae knew the elderly woman would not be able to handle the stairs leading up to the loft.

I should add there are two ways of reaching the loft apartment. One way of course is from the outside and the other the other is from inside the house's family room. The family room is an add on to the main house. The Arizona room, Laundry room and Pantry are also in this section of the house.

The main part of Mae's home is the Kitchen, TV room, a nook with a Linen closet, Mae's room and what was at the time my room. It a pretty big house. You go through a heavy curtain to the other part of the house and besides the Quest Bathroom I forgot to mention is a spiral staircase that leads up to the loft. It is a hard-wooden staircase and very narrow. Easy for an older person to fall down.

Mae eventually asked me if I would take the loft apartment. I was thrilled at first. My own living space. It seemed ideal. The loft has its own tiny bathroom, (Just a toilet and sink), a little nook for cooking, my own way inside or out. The only thing I did not like was all the windows. Mae liked windows, every door but one was made of glass, every room had many windows. I honestly did not like the idea of having virtually wall to wall windows but my tiny wooden door.

I put up huge, thick blankets over some of the windows. I found an old screen and placed it over the large one by the door. I blocked other with a modest, light armoire. I felt secured with these items in place. I did not want any peeping toms!

Mrs. Edwards seemed like a nice woman at first. She had been polite during her interview and expressed her heartfelt thanks upon moving in. She appeared to be a little off to me right away. I do not think either Mae or I had suspect what a truly awful human being she would turn out to be.

Mrs. Edwards had been with us about a month when her true nature emerged. The woman was a nightmare in her own right. She was continuously insulting to Mae. The woman was putting her down all the time, cussing at her, demanding, and just a general pain in the ass.

One night I was sound asleep when the sound of her screaming woke me with a start. It took a few moments to organize my thoughts. I heard her screams of terror again and tore down the stairs.

"What is wrong?" I demanded storming into her room.

Mrs. Edwards eyes were huge like sauces, she was shaking violently and for once her voice came in a broken whisper. "Out the window." She barely got out pointing towards the bigger of the two windows in her room.

I strolled over to the window and looked out. "I don't see anything." I told her after a few seconds of scanning the outside.

"It was there." She insisted. "Call the police they need to know."

"What was there?" I question holding her. It was clear she saw something. She was more than passively frighten.

"Call them now!" She demanded more like herself, shoving me away.

I went into the kitchen and grabbed the phone calling the non-emergency number to the police.

I explained the situation and less than 6 minutes later a policeman was knocking on the door. I moved to let him in.

"I looked around the house there does not seem to be a prowler of any kind." He greeted me. "All I saw was a very quiet owl, just off to the right of the house."

"Well thank you Officer." I comment shaking his hand, "I appreciate you coming out so late."

Mrs. Edwards came out of her room. She was wearing just her pull ups due to the hot weather. I blushed a deep red noting the Officer's discomfort.

"I know what I saw young man." Pointing her shiny, boney, finger at him.

The Officer recovered quickly from his shock and motioned for her to sit down. Mrs. Edwards took a seat on the couch and he in the chair catty -cornered,

He took out his note pad asked her name and other relevant information. He then did the same of me. "Now can you describe what this prowler looked like?" he asked.

"It was a werewolf with reddish eyes staring in my window." She told him dead serious. "I got up to go to the bathroom and when I came back there it was staring at me through my window."

The Officer did not believe her of course, but I did! The next morning, I went out to have a look under her window for tracks. I found them. I wear a size six shoe in women, these tracks were bigger. They were also from a very, large wolf. The most horrific thing I noted that morning…. Both window screens had been shredded to pieces!

Chapter Seven: Just a Door Between Us

This night will forever haunt me. The sheer reality of staring

certain death in the eye. There are no words to describe that kind of

fear. It resonate through your entire being. You cannot breathe,

move, you feel at the mercy of a cruel and uncertain fate. You

know you have just become the prey.

Human being are an apex predator in their own right. There are

several creatures out there who hunt us as a source of an easy meal.

Sometimes we hunt those apex predators and sometimes we are the

hunters and they our prey. We kill more shark every year than

shark kill us. We kill more bears, Cougars, Coyotes etc... I cannot

phantom a single human being that would hunt one of these things

unless they were forced too.

Mae and I had stayed up late one night watching old movies. It

amused her to no end how much I enjoyed some of the classic. I

genuinely love a great western. My all-time favorites are still "War

Wagon." "The Villain" and "McClintock,". This night were had a blast watching "Arsenic and Old Lace." Mae thought I would enjoy it and I did immensely.

It was somewhere between 12 am and 1am when I headed up the staircase to bed. I thought to have one more smoke before turning in. I had just step outside into the Summer heat and I heard something coming hard and fast up the tree near the terrace. I jumped back into the house, slammed the door tight, flip the lock and threw the bolt.

I expected to hear the sounds of a Mountain lion or Bobcat, nothing could have prepared me for what I did hear. It was unholy! I backed away from the door and sat on my bed frozen in terror. The sound was very wolf -like. It was howling, huffing, scratching at the door and it was so pissed off. I mean this thing sounded aggressive, and massive.

I had to know what was making that horrible sounds. I inched over to the lower part of the window and what I saw sent my body into a state of numb intimidation, dismay, and shock. My mind could not accept this thing was very much real. A werewolf!

Its head was like a German Shepherd's or Wolf's, bulky, body held the hugest muscles of any creature on land I had ever saw, it was covered in black and silver fur. It Paws were not paws, but hands with shape looking nails (surely for ripping prey apart), but its hind legs were that of any other Canines.

I watched transfixed as it began to throw things from the porch.
It tossed my chair first, then my table, the monster shatter a mirror
I had out there. In a short while (Though it felt much longer)
everything out there on the porch was tossed to the ground below.

It must have sensed me watching It because the Creature turned
back to the window. It Yellow eyes watched me through the glass.
I was confused the one I saw on the road had red eyes. Was it some
kind of trick of the full moon or the loft's lighting? Those eyes
seemed to glow like a cats. It moved eye level to me. Literally we
were eye to eye just the glass between us. I peed myself. It smirked
at me and jumped off the porch.

I stayed awake all night waiting for it to return. It did not. The
next day, I cleaned up the mess and told not a single soul what had
happened. The following night, it came to the door again. I cried
from the bed unable to process why this monster was hounding me.
I started sleeping downstairs on the couch.

I took extra care with the house too to protect the three of us. I
installed all new doors and deadbolt for every possible way in. I
put locks on all the windows. I brought my first rifle and learned to
shoot it. This was my home not that things.

The Creature continued to come around the house until fall. In
fall the being just vanished. It felt safe again. We all breathed
much easier. Then Winter came and the terror returned announcing

itself with a bloody, throat ripped out deer on our back part of the porch near the dog's kennel.

I was back into my own room by then. Mrs. Edwards was forcibly removed from the home after she attacked Mae with a butch knife. The police did not lock her up. It was believed to be an act of pure confusion. Whatever it was, Mae spent two weeks in the hospital recovering. I took the dogs and went to William's.

Mae and I began to hear footsteps across our roof every night. It terrified both of us. She refused to believe the possible it was anything other than a skunk. The footsteps sounded human to me, not animal. I was convinced that someone was trying to break into our home. I took the rifle up the stairs late one night and found it was our Wolfie friend making that noise. It did not see me this time. I am sure it would not have liked the rifle in my hands. I am not sure I could use it or would have gotten a chance too.

The last straw for me was the dead Mountain Lion I found on the edge of our land. I was heading back to get Mae, turned back where it had been, and it was gone. It never once occurred to me that this werewolf like creature came out during the day light hours. The reality was more than I could bare. I told Mae we either need to tell someone or I was leaving. I moved back to Phoenix a week later.

An interesting foot note here: All the troubles stop once I moved. It made me wonder if the Creature had been staking me all along.

This all began after I saw it on the road that night. Had I somehow angered it just by seeing it? Did it catch my sent? I am "Fun Size "prey. I probably looked like easy prey too.

Chapter Eight: Dogman Having Fun

My friend Noah related this tale his Dad Adam and he experienced just outside of Munds Park Arizona. The two had gone on what would be one of their last fishing trips. The place where they went fishing Noah says is very secluded. It was just a private fishing whole they came across on a hunting trip years earlier.

"Dad and I were excited we had caught our limited and were looking forwards to a nice fish fry." Noah related to me the memory dancing over his face. 'It had been one of the best days Dad and I had ever shared. I treasure it to this day Dad died so soon afterwards. "He gave a little chuckle even though we had a turn of luck and the crap scared out of us."

Noah's face grew more sober as he continued. "I had nodded off to sleep. It had been a long, hot Summer's day in August, and it was about 2 am. I drove the first part of our trip home." Noah informed me as his tale grew. "Dad had taken over for me just outside of Flagstaff like I said I had chilled out and fallen asleep."

The area where this encounter took place is in the pines, meadow, ranches, desert scrubs, oaks, elms. It one of the most forest places in Arizona. The weather even in Summer is somewhat mild, especially compared to the rest of the state. The Mogollon Rim is remarkably similar. Both regions are known for their monster activities.

Noah continued his retelling of his story. I asked for as much detail as he could remember. "I woke suddenly." He told me "It was as if something was just off." I could tell he was getting a tad upset on this point. "I looked around and in the side mirror I saw a huge, wolf- like being, on two legs, running alongside our truck." He stated

Somehow this made sense to me. Dogs run beside cars all the time. This is just their way of saying this is my place or maybe it is just their way of having a bit of fun. It been reported that dogs do this due to loneliness or instincts, perhaps curious and other say they may have had a bad experience with the driver. There is also just the fun of the chase.

"Dad, Dad/" I remember calling as the werewolf was gaining speed on us. I looked over to see my Dad was driving around 65 miles per hour.

My Dad turned his head turned to answer my pleads. "Werewolf!" He cried pointing right outside my window. I unbuckled my seatbelt and flew over to the driver's side as fast as I could.

"Can you tell me what it looked like to you, in your own words." I suggested encouraging him to finish his recounting.

"It was running on it back legs, its arms were out in front of it," He tried to remember as much details as possible. 'It looked like a true to life Werewolf." He could not say more

Noah's encounter lasted over twenty miles. Noah and his father lost their travel mate near a rest area just outside of where they lived in Cornville. The two carefully exited their truck, not bothering to unpack. They were grateful for ditching their chasing friend and just wanted to get inside.

The next morning (afternoon), Noah went to empty the fish from the cooler they had placed them in. The cooler was empty. All their gear had been gone through, some was broken, and others were found on the ground. Noah looked around, He froze all around the small house and truck were large wolf prints.

Chapter Nine: Food for Thought

This book is more non-fiction than fictions, however it was important for the telling to change certain events to add a sense of security to the people in the story. One person has since died. The rest did not want their real names or in some cases the actual locations of their encounters exposed.

My own experiences happened as I said they did in Arizona. The two encounters left me paralyzed with an unspeakable fear. I just could not wrap my mind around a Werewolf like creature.  After my second encounter I began to look for answers online and found Dogman Encounter.com I searched through every story. I then found a story so much like what I experienced in the loft that night, just reading the story created the same agonizing horror. Remembering the only thing that was between us was a door. A flimsy, thin, door This monster size being of nearly seven feet tall could have smashed in easily. It weighed enough to collapse a portion of the porch. It must have weight at least three - hundred pounds if not more. These beast should not be messed with.

I continue to research the Dogman to this day. Some of the stories I have read leave me wondering just how long these beings have been around? If they are supernatural or of nature? I heard more than one claim that they are a Bioweapon of our government. The sighting go back too far for this to be true.

I know there are hot spots of Dogman activity. The most Notable ones are "Beast of Bray Road.", The Michigan Dogman and in Staffordshire County England tales of "Old Stinker" and "The Beast of Bramston"

I have heard of unexplained animal death as well. Death were the attacking animals could not be clearly defined beyond the fact they were of a canine breed, just not a known ones. I want to leave you with this, we as human being have bred at least thirty-four different breeds of Dog from Wolves. What has nature itself bred.

About the Author

Christyne Anne is a wife of twenty-seven years and mother of four sons Larry, Joshua, Jefferson, and James. She lives in Arizona with her family.

Christyne Anne is the head writer and founder of The Purple Rose Website for Akathisia education. The site also features Recovery, Covid 19 information, recipes, and pictures from her many adventures. She is an Emergency Medical Technician by trade and Psychology student.

Christyne Anne loves being outdoors rather it be camping, hiking, horseback riding, fishing, or swimming. She enjoys writing, cooking, ceramic and crafting in her down time.

You can write her at christyneanne1@gmail.com. Please feel free to share your own tales of the supernatural.

---

www.ingramcontent.com/pod-product-compliance
Lightning Source LLC
Chambersburg PA
CBHW061717130726
47996CB00006B/2370